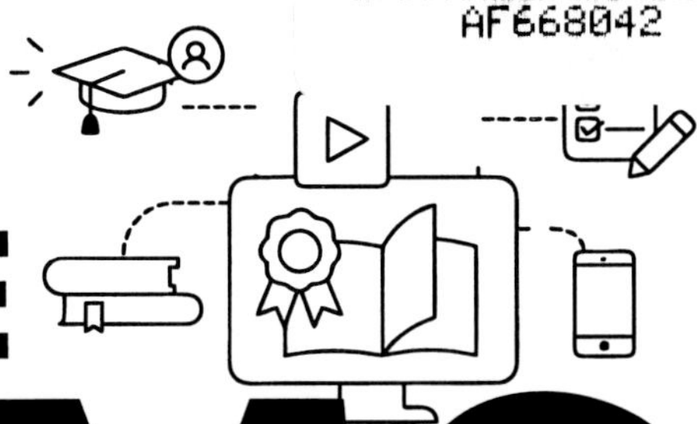

THE LMS BLUEPRINT

THE LMS BLUEPRINT

GUNJAN GUPTA

Available on amazonkindle

Worldwide Published by

Pendown Press

PREMIUM BUSINESS PUBLISHER

PENDOWN PRESS LLP

An ISO 9001 & ISO 14001 Certified Co.,

Regd. Office: 3767A, Kanhaiya Nagar,

Tri Nagar, Delhi-110035

Ph.: 8130886000, 9650072927

E-mail: info@pendownpress.com

Branch Office: 1A/2A, 20, Hari Sadan, Ansari Road,

Daryaganj, New Delhi-110002

Ph.: 011-45794768

Website: PendownPress.com

Edition: 2025

Price: ₹ 499

ISBN: 978-93-7217-322-2

Layout and Cover Designed by Pendown Graphics Team

Disclaimer

Everything in this book comes from real conversations, real challenges, and real lessons I've seen over the years working closely with L&D and HR teams. While I've avoided naming specific companies or disclosing confidential details, the examples and frameworks are drawn from the kind of situations most corporates face when implementing an LMS.

This book is meant to guide you, not to prescribe one-size-fits-all answers.

Your context, your people, and your challenges will shape what works for you. Use this as a playbook, adapt it to your needs, and when in doubt, ask questions, seek advice, and trust your instincts as an L&D leader.

No vendor is endorsed here, and no strategy is guaranteed. The goal is to help you ask the right questions and avoid expensive mistakes before you commit.

Learning platforms, LMS, and LXP are used interchangeably. I may have used different words to communicate different emotions where appropriate. This is intentional.

Table of Contents

Chapter 2: Buying & Setting Up the Right LMS

Preface

Before anything else, I want to say thank you.

Thank you for picking up this book. Thank you for giving Learning is a journey we all begin long before we realize it. Some of us discover it in classrooms, some at work, and many during the unexpected turns of life. My own journey in Learning & Development has been shaped by curiosity, mistakes, meaningful conversations and a deep belief that learning can truly change how people grow, succeed, and feel valued.

Over the last 26 years in L&D, I've seen learning through many lenses: as a learner myself (because I still love learning), as a trainer, as someone running LMS platforms, as a manager leading over 1000 people over the years, as a founder building an L&D-driven organization, and as a partner to corporates trying to bridge the gap between HR's expectations and the end user's real needs.

Between 1999 and 2006, while working with Aptech Ltd. and Lionbridge (a Nasdaq-listed company), something important became clear to me: India needed its own solutions, built not just for compliance or content delivery, but for true experience, scale, and learning impact.

That insight became a mission. A mission to help organizations, in India and globally, unlock learning that actually solves problems, empowers people, and drives growth. Not what global tools think we should need, but what we know we need.

Now, I'm writing this book because it allows me to reach more people faster, with insights that are hard-earned and field-tested.

This is not just another LMS guide. It's a blueprint you can use to implement learning platforms with clarity and confidence, avoiding the common mistakes, and aligning learning with business growth.

A First Gift for You

If you're holding this book, you already have a seat at the table.

Take a picture with the book and email it to ***theLMSblueprint@violetinfo.ai*** and my team will onboard you into an exclusive community of L&D leaders who are shaping the future of learning.

I'm here to support your journey. **Let's build something meaningful and impactful together.**

Acknowledgements

Every journey is shaped by the people who walk beside us, sometimes visibly, sometimes quietly in the background. Mine is no different.

Where I am today wouldn't be possible without you all.

To my parents, your love, trust, and quiet strength shaped not just my values, but the foundation of how I live and lead each day.

To my partner in life and business, **Rhea** and our beloved son, **Om**, thank you for being my compass, my clarity, and my constant source of balance. You've seen the unfiltered version of this journey and still cheered me on.

To my mentors, **Neeraj Shah, Rahul Jain,** and **Akshar Yadav,** and to everyone whose questions, insights, or challenges pushed me to grow, thank you for sharpening my thinking. Your influence runs through these pages.

To **Vivek Gokhale, Udit Bhatia, Amrita Mohanty, Premal Pipalia, Mrinal Mohan** and every customer who placed their trust in me, thank you for your belief, your challenges and your partnership. You helped turn real experiences into real insights. This book exists because of you.

To **my team** at Zobble and Violet Info, thanks for standing by me and believing in me. This journey would not have been possible without your relentless effort and commitment.

Last but not least, to **Mr. Dinesh Verma** and his publishing house, Pendown Press, your skill, care, and attention to detail have transformed these words into a book I am proud of. Thank you for bringing this project to life with such commitment.

Thank you for shaping not just this book, but the blueprint of my journey.

Who This Book Is For?

This book is for HR professionals who lead or support Learning and Development.

It's for those who:

- **Dream big for learning:** You want your team to thrive, not just tick boxes.
- **Take action:** Whether it's your first L&D project or your hundredth, you want it done right.
- **Avoid pitfalls:** You're tired of costly mistakes and dead-end tools.

If this is you, welcome. This book will be your practical guide to creating a system that truly supports your team and organization.

How to Use This Book?

This book isn't theory. It's everything I've learned from being in your shoes, sometimes running, sometimes firefighting, and often trying to make sense of conflicting priorities around learning.

Volume 1 is about getting it right before you even begin, not just launching an LMS.

No dashboards. No feature comparisons. Just the groundwork, making sure you don't end up with a tool no one uses, or worse, a decision you regret.

Use this book in whatever way serves you best. L&D leaders can get value from it at different stages:

- **If you're planning to buy an LMS:** Start from the first chapter. Don't skip. You'll find the questions you didn't even know you needed to ask, both internally and externally.
- **If you're trying to get leadership buy-in:** Focus on the sections about pitching the LMS to your CEO, CFO, CHRO, and others. I've broken down what each of them wants to hear and how you can communicate it with confidence.
- **If your current LMS feels like a mistake:** This book will help you understand what should have been done. Even

if you haven't implemented everything yet, it will make it easier to reflect and correct your course of action.

- **If you're stuck between multiple vendors:** Refer to the vendor evaluation and hidden traps chapters. They'll save you time, budget, and a lot of unnecessary drama.
- **Not sure if your organization is culturally ready?** Jump to the section on building a learning culture before bringing in technology. Because the best LMS in the world won't work if the environment isn't ready to support it. You'll find clear signs to watch out for, and guidance on what to fix before you invest.

Keep this book handy. Bookmark the checklists. Highlight the parts that feel like your story. And when you feel stuck, come back to it.

This isn't a book you read once and forget. It's the one you keep nearby when you're in the middle of decisions that matter. And if you need help or want to discuss your situation, don't hesitate to reach out.

Introduction:
The Blueprint

Every structure stands tall because of what's underneath, its blueprint.

This book began with a simple realisation: most LMS projects don't fail because of only bad software. They fail because the foundation was never clearly laid out.

Timelines often dominate before clarity is even established.

Decisions get made before the right questions are even asked. What I've shared here is not just a list of steps. It's a field-tested plan, drawn from the ground realities of implementing learning platforms in real organizations, with real constraints, across roles, functions, and regions.

This is the part most people skip, and it's the part that makes the biggest difference.

So before you start reading the book, take a moment to shift your mindset. Don't treat this like a product decision. Treat it like an architectural one. You're not just buying software.

You're shaping how your organization learns, adapts, and grows.

And solid outcomes are never accidental; they are built through a blueprint.

That is exactly what this book gives you:

The LMS Blueprint.

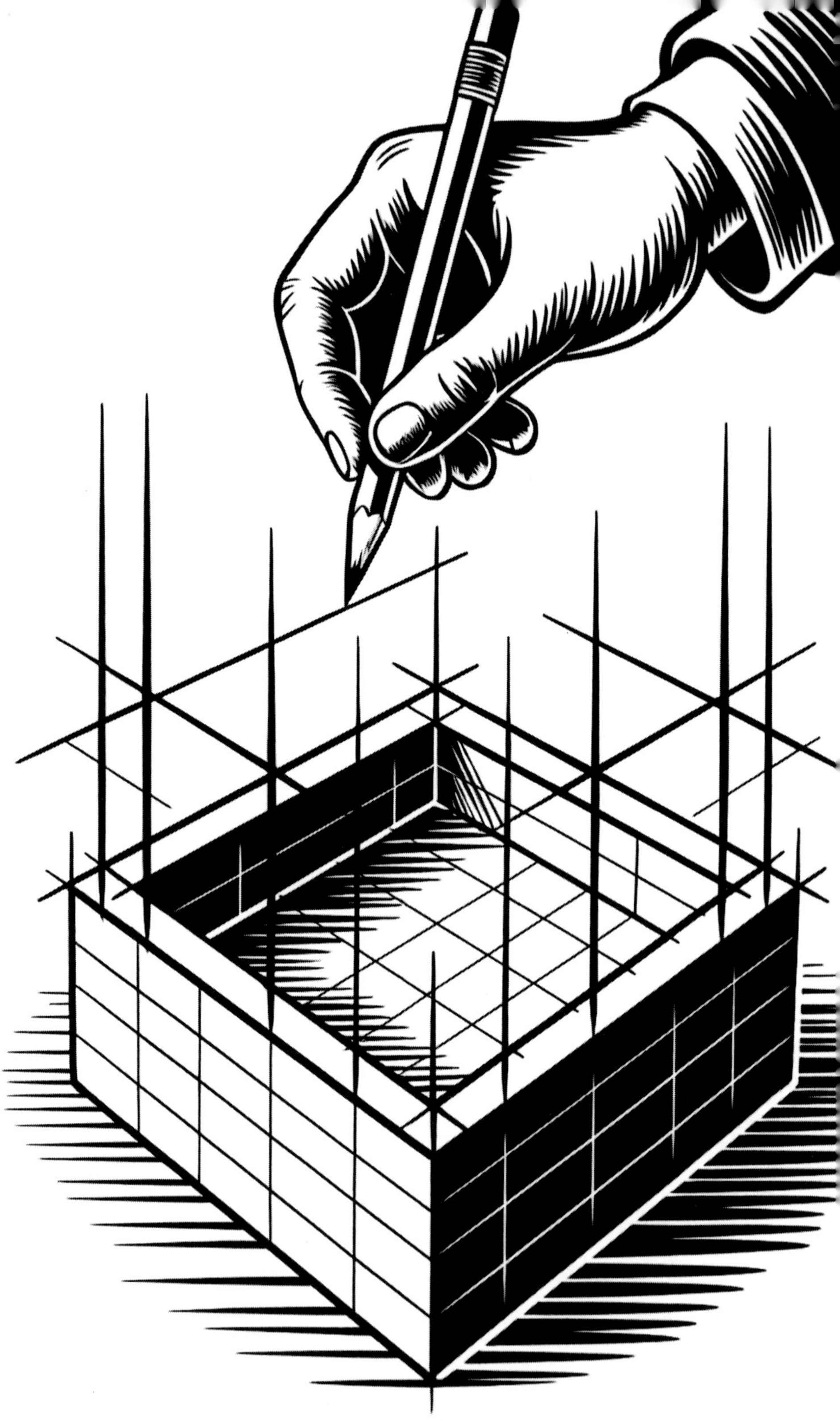

Chapter

01

Building the Case & Getting the Basics Right

Over the years, I've seen many LMS projects go off track, not because the tools were bad, but because the basics were overlooked. Sometimes, assessments weren't done, priorities weren't clear, or the groundwork wasn't laid properly. These gaps often lead to wasted time, frustration, and results that fall short of expectations.

Before diving into features, dashboards, or vendors, it's crucial to step back and understand why an LMS is needed in the first place. This chapter will help you assess your current learning ecosystem, identify cracks, and make informed decisions before moving forward.

DO I REALLY NEED AN LMS?

1.1 "Do I really need an LMS?"

Spotting the Cracks in Your Learning Ecosystem

If your current training plan feels more like a never-ending struggle than a smooth operation, it's time to pause and reassess. You might be putting in a lot of time and energy to get your employees trained, but still not seeing the results you hoped for. This isn't uncommon, many organizations face similar challenges and sometimes the root cause is less obvious than it seems.

The real question is: **Is your training program truly hitting its goals, or is there something holding it back that's hard to pinpoint?** It might not be about the effort you're putting in, but rather about needing a system that can help bring structure and clarity to your training efforts.

Here's how you can tell if it's time to consider an LMS: (Tick the checkboxes)

- ☐ **Your employees are spread across multiple locations:** Coordinating training across different regions feels like running in circles. Each location might be conducting its own training, leading to inconsistent learning experiences.
- ☐ **New hires are joining with different roles every month:** It's a challenge to provide tailored onboarding for each of them, and they might be left to navigate on their own without a structured process.

- ☐ **Managers are too busy to focus on training sessions:** Their calendars are always packed, and training tends to get deprioritized. As a result, sessions are inconsistent and lacking in impact.
- ☐ **Your industry demands a high level of expertise and continuous learning:** If you're in finance, IT, or any other sector that requires employees to keep up with evolving knowledge, it's tough to manage without a system that ensures everyone stays current.
- ☐ **Your products or services keep changing:** Each new launch or update means retraining your team. If you don't have an effective way to roll out this training quickly, you risk creating knowledge gaps that can affect service quality.
- ☐ **High employee turnover is a regular occurrence:** When people leave faster than you can onboard them, you need an efficient training system that gets new hires up to speed quickly and effectively.
- ☐ **Your business follows a seasonal cycle:** When your workforce scales up or down during peak seasons, your training needs to be able to adapt accordingly. Handling this without a robust system, results in missed opportunities for skill-building.
- ☐ **Different locations, different languages:** Your branches may need training material in multiple languages, making it hard to ensure consistency and relevance without a centralized system.
- ☐ **Finding good trainers is always a struggle:** Even if you manage to find the right trainers, coordinating in-person sessions is time-consuming and costly. And when they leave, all that expertise leaves with them.

☐ **Training-related travel costs are through the roof:** If you're spending a fortune moving people around for training, it's time to rethink how you deliver learning. Costs shouldn't be that high just to get the right content to the right people.

If you find yourself **ticking two or more of these points, it's a sign** that there might be deeper challenges with your training approach. Compliance gaps, widening skill gaps, and employees feeling overwhelmed are clear indicators that the current setup might not be addressing your needs effectively. This doesn't mean your efforts are wasted; it just means a more structured solution could be what's needed to bring everything together.

Imagine this scenario: It's time for an annual compliance review, and you discover that many employees haven't completed the required training. Now, you're at risk of non-compliance issues, potential penalties, and a difficult conversation with senior management.

Or, perhaps there's a sudden change in regulations, and your employees missed out on the necessary updates because there wasn't a streamlined way to get everyone trained in time.

An LMS can bring order to the chaos.

It helps you centralize training, track progress in real time, and ensure information and actions do not slip through the cracks. Automated reminders, easy access to training content, and instant reporting mean that when it's time to show results, you'll have everything you need at your fingertips.

So, before you find yourself facing these challenges again, ask yourself: **Is an LMS the solution you need to take control of your training and turn it into a strategic advantage?**

KNOW YOUR AUDIENCE

1.2 KYA – Know Your Audience

Understanding Learner

It is important that you understand your audience with different parameters:

- Learning styles
- Individual and team workload
- Environmental limitations
- Technology savviness
- Language barriers
- Preferred learning mediums

The Covid-19 pandemic demonstrated our capacity for adaptation, but today's L&D transformation efforts require voluntary buy-in, not forced compliance.

> *"If someone is used to a certain way of learning, it is your job to ensure that they learn and that you create a conducive environment."*
>
> ~ **Gunjan Gupta**

Segment Your Learners

Your audience isn't homogeneous. Field workers, factory teams, corporate staff, each engages differently and reacts to learning in their own way. For example, a factory worker might prefer short, visual, hands-on modules, while a corporate professional may engage better with longer, discussion-based sessions or self-paced e-learning.

Phasing the rollout by function, tech access, and language ensures personalized experiences. It's the difference between a "Generic LMS" and an "LMS for All."

Language Is Your First Barrier

The language of the platform can become a major barrier if the audience isn't comfortable with English. Even when the content is localized, the interface alone can discourage users who are more comfortable in their native language.

Consider multilingual options, subtitles, or simplified interfaces to reduce friction. Training adoption increases significantly when learners feel the platform "speaks their language", literally. Providing culturally and linguistically appropriate support also signals respect for your workforce, making them more likely to embrace learning rather than see it as a compliance task.

TIMING IT RIGHT

When to pull the trigger
on an LMS

1.3 Timing It Right: When to Pull the Trigger on an LMS

Just because you feel the pain doesn't mean you're ready for surgery. The same logic applies to launching an LMS. Needing one is one thing. Being ready to implement it successfully is a whole other game.

Many organizations jump in simply because someone at the top says, *"Let's go digital."* But here's the catch: they often dive in without checking if the ground is even ready to support it. Rushing an LMS rollout without proper readiness almost always backfires.

Let's break it down.

When You Shouldn't Wait Any Longer

If you're launching tons of training programs annually and still using Excel to track attendance, you're not managing training; you're one step away from a disaster.

If auditors are throwing non-compliance flags at you, that's not just a red alert, it's a siren. This isn't the phase where you ask, *"Should we consider an LMS?"* This is the phase where you ask, *"How soon can we go live?"*

Timing Must Align with Business Rhythms

LMS implementation isn't something you slap onto the business calendar randomly. Implementing during appraisal season, sales peak, or a major organizational shift? Recipe for disaster. People are already maxed out, and your LMS will feel like an unnecessary interruption.

Ideally, launch it just before the start of your financial year. That gives you a full year of clean data and better planning.

For companies on an April-March cycle, a Jan-March implementation works well. But ultimately, timing depends on your business rhythm, and ignoring that will require more effort than the usual to get adoption in the initial phase.

If you miss the ideal time or you have defined timelines to go live, then just prepare well and ask for buffer time to evaluate the success of the platform (adoption and completions). Your LMS needs breathing space. Start during a calmer period, resource it fully, and be visible with leadership support.

> *"Don't treat LMS as a checklist item you can implement anytime. It has to align with your business cycle to deliver real outcomes."*
>
> ~ **Gunjan Gupta**

THE LEARNING CULTURE SHIFT

1.4 The Learning Culture Shift

You Are Not Just Buying A Software

Buying an LMS isn't a tech decision; it's a transformative shift. You're not just installing software, you're redesigning how your company learns, tracks, and grows. You're replacing manuals, papers, and spreadsheets with real-time tracking and actionable insights.

This change touches every layer: trainers need training, coordinators need tools, leaders need clarity, and employees need to adopt a new way of learning. Without culture alignment, even the most sophisticated LMS can struggle to deliver its potential.

Learning Cultural Reality Check

Whether you're starting fresh or upgrading an existing system, success depends not just on the licenses or features you purchase, it depends equally on mindset and culture.

> *"Without learning culture alignment, even the best LMS won't survive"*
>
> ~ **Gunjan Gupta**

Learning culture is not an outcome of one person or generalised statement for all employees. There are different aspects of learning culture that needs to be understood to bring the change.

❖ Learner Mindset

Introducing digital learning in a company accustomed to five-star training venues and buffet lunches requires careful expectation management. Don't expect applause when rolling out online modules, resistance won't be about content; it will be about the learning experience they're losing.

Moving from classroom training with in-person energy to solo e-learning can feel like a downgrade. People will resist, even if they don't say so. Feedback like, *"The video didn't load,"* or *"I didn't get time"* are signals, often silent ones.

❖ Top Management

In smaller companies or organizations where digital is still "optional," resistance isn't merely emotional; it's foundational. Top leaders must understand why learning matters, or the initiative will struggle from the start.

❖ Managers/Heads of Department

If managers themselves don't believe in learning, it becomes nearly impossible to get their support for a learning platform. And it's not always resistance. It could be delivery pressure, packed schedules, or simply not knowing how critical learning is to long-term performance. Some believe that the way they learnt in the past, through trial and error, is how the next generation should learn too. But that approach doesn't always work in today's fast-changing environment.

> *"Change management in L&D is a war against human behavior. It starts with changing mindsets, then habits, and finally, making them believe in what's important."*
>
> **~ Gunjan Gupta**

- **Start With the First 10**

  Focus on inviting the top layer, digital advocates, early adopters, and team leaders who can influence the culture. Don't try to spread too thin.

Change Management Sutra

> *"One man can motivate tens, which can motivate hundreds, which can motivate thousands. So know your ten, the first ten, and involve them early."*
>
> **~ Gunjan Gupta**

Show them the possibilities, let them explore, and let them reflect. This group becomes the anchor for widespread adoption. Train them well, involve them in decisions, and make them champions of the change.

While selecting these members, focus on those who have grown, evolved, and are not stagnant in their learning journey. (I am sure 100% of these were learners).

Remember: Not everyone needs a book to learn. Some people absorb knowledge by doing, trying things they've never done before, and pushing beyond their comfort zone. These early adopters are your key to embedding a learning culture that sticks.

INVEST INTO
CONTENT

1.5 Invest Into Content

Common Mistake: Copy-Pasting Global Content

Sharing courses from Udemy, Coursera, Percipio, LinkedIn Learning sounds like a quick win, until you realize your employees don't connect with the language, context, or pace. If the content feels alien, adoption drops. People won't say it's bad; they just won't come back.

You're not just buying content. You need the right content that fits your audience.

Example: Using US-centric financial compliance modules in Indian BFSI context may cause disconnect. Or, if your audience isn't comfortable with English, purchasing content that's not only in English but also accented may leave it largely unused.

Gun With No Bullets Will Leave You Dead

When you buy a gun, you need to have the bullets. The right bullets made for those you plan to hunt. You guessed it right, here the gun is the LMS, the bullets are your content and the hunted is actually your learner.

Though this analogy may backfire but this is the easiest way to explain that having one without the other is useless. It also shows that you need to know what you are up against to understand which kind of bullets will work.

This is where most organizations go wrong. They either invest in a platform without knowing what they'll upload, or they have content scattered across folders but no engine to deliver it at scale.

LMS
ARE YOU READY TO BEGIN
LMS VENDOR EVALUATION?

1.6 Are You Ready To Begin LMS Vendor Evaluation?

These points help you assess whether you're ready to engage with LMS providers *without wasting time or budget.*

- ☐ **Leadership Buy-In:** Your CXOs and CHRO are not just aware, they're aligned and willing to support.
- ☐ **Defined Use Cases:** You've clearly identified 3–5 high-impact learning needs (e.g. onboarding, compliance, functional training).
- ☐ **Budget Preparedness:** You have financial approval or clarity on how the budget will be allocated for platform + content + setup.
- ☐ **Internal Team:** You have a named project owner, and ideally, a cross-functional team (HR, IT, L&D) in place.
- ☐ **Tech Integration Considerations:** You know what systems (HRMS, SSO, email, content partners) the LMS will need to integrate with.
- ☐ **Data Hygiene:** Basic, clean user data (departments, roles, locations, employee IDs) is ready, or there's a clear plan to clean it.
- ☐ **Content Audit Done:** You've reviewed what training materials already exist and what needs to be created or bought.

- [ ] **Rollout Timeline Agreed:** There's an internal sense of when this project will go live, and how long you can invest in the setup phase.

If you tick **5 or more**, you're ready to begin vendor conversations. If you tick less than 4, pause and prepare, or risk a rollout with poor adoption and high regret.

PITCH IT
LIKE A PRO

1.7 "Pitch It Like A Pro"

Showing Real ROI

When making the case for an LMS, it's critical to challenge the misconception that Learning & Development (L&D) doesn't generate revenue. Think of L&D as parallel to marketing.

Just as marketing is an investment that indirectly drives sales, L&D is an investment that fuels operational excellence, compliance, and customer satisfaction. It ensures that every employee, no matter their role or location, delivers the level of quality and service that defines your brand.

Presenting L&D as a **value-add** that reinforces the brand's promise and enables the organization to operate at its best.

It's not about *"If we do this, what's the revenue gain?"* but rather, *"If we don't do this, what's at stake?"*

Here's how to position L&D as an indispensable part of the business:

- **L&D as a Quality Enabler**: Training is what ensures consistent quality across all operations, guaranteeing that customers receive the same level of service and product knowledge wherever they interact with your brand. It's this consistency that solidifies brand trust and loyalty, something that can't always be measured directly but is invaluable in maintaining a competitive edge.
- **Align L&D as a Risk mitigator**: Emphasize that L&D safeguards the integrity of the brand by reducing incidents of non-compliance, mis-selling, or poor customer service. It's an investment that not only shields the company from reputational risk but also upholds the brand's standard of excellence. Highlight the impact of

errors that could have been prevented through effective training and assessments.

- **Investment, Not Expense**: Just as marketing drives brand recognition, L&D drives competency and quality. Positioning it this way will help you communicate that cutting corners in training is equivalent to underfunding marketing, both have long-term consequences that can damage the brand.
- **ROI Beyond Sales**: Present metrics that go beyond immediate revenue. Consider metrics such as customer satisfaction scores, employee retention rates, and compliance rates. Show that without L&D, these areas would likely suffer, which in turn could lead to lost customers, higher turnover costs, and increased risk of compliance issues.

What's In It for Them? Aligning the LMS to Business Goals

Make your LMS look like a strategic win, not an expense line for:

- CEO/Founder
- CFO
- CHRO
- CTO
- Procurement

Let's deep dive for each profile.

❖ **CEO or Founders**

When speaking to the CEO or founders, the following three objectives must be expanded into an actionable plan. It's not just about convincing them; it's about selecting a platform that can confidently deliver on the promised outcomes.

- **Internal and External Brand Building**: CEOs or founders see learning as more than just a software implementation. When you position the platform as an *"academy"* rather than just a *"Learning Management System,"* it resonates with their long-term vision. *"Academy"* evokes a sense of purpose, while *"LMS"* sounds transactional.
- **Internal Brand**: A learning academy can inspire internal stakeholders and reflect a company culture focused on employee growth, rather than just workload. It conveys a forward-looking vision that founders want to champion.
- **External Brand**: Founders are also interested in how the academy will strengthen the organization's external positioning. They may use it in investor presentations, customer communication, or personal branding to highlight a strong learning culture.
- **Business Continuity Plan & Big Audacious Goal plan:** CEOs or founders have the responsibility to keep the business running no matter what. What if there is a mass resignation? What if key stakeholders resign/ not available? What if we bag a great deal and need to upscale, how will we hire and train so many people? How can we train them to maintain quality with consistency so they can start doing the job in half the time?

- **CFO**

CFOs are driven by Return on Investment (ROI), cost-effective implementations, and risk mitigation.

- **Company's Interest at Both Ends**: They will typically try to negotiate terms to secure the organization's interests. Contracts may include clauses that de-risk the investment. Be open to listening to them and helping negotiate critical terms that matter.
- **The Whole Cost**: Putting upfront the recurring and one time cost will matter a lot in decision making.
- **Risk Mitigation**: Present evidence of due diligence, product trials, demos, comparison reports, evaluation scorecards, and ROI analysis. Showcase both direct and indirect benefits to build confidence in your recommendation. Cost justification and the rationale behind choosing a particular vendor are critical. You should also clearly explain why you did not choose the lowest-cost option.

- **CHRO**

CHROs manage a broad spectrum of HR functions and must see the LMS as more than just a training tool. It is important to pitch it in a way that shows how everything in HR can be tied together within one system. But always understand what is important for the CHROs or what is important for the organization and then pitch the LMS with specific rational.

If you are the CHRO, please read through this to identify clear areas where you can make an impact and leave a lasting legacy for the evolution of the organization by creating content beyond just technical skills.

HR Function	Key Areas	Sample Content Topics
Talent Acquisition	Sourcing, Screening, Interviewing, Offer Management	Effective Interviewing Skills, DEI in Hiring, Employer Branding
Onboarding	Pre-boarding, Induction, Role Orientation, Culture Assimilation	Understanding Company Culture, Compliance Induction, Buddy Program Essentials
Learning & Development	Skill Building, Leadership Development, Learning Paths, Mentorship	Learning to Learn, Leadership Essentials, Time Management, Digital Fluency
Performance Management	Goal Setting, Feedback, Appraisals, Performance Reviews	Performance Feedback Training, Goal Setting Workshops, Constructive Conversations
Competency Management	Competency Mapping, Skill Gap Analysis, Growth Frameworks	Skill Assessment Tools, Creating Learning Journeys, Role Benchmarking
Succession Planning	HiPo Identification, Talent Pool Development, Role Readiness	Career Growth Conversations, HiPo Readiness Programs, Leadership Grooming

Employee Engagement	Rewards & Recognition, Career Growth, Continuous Feedback	Employee Motivation, Recognition Frameworks, Career Progression Tracks
Compensation & Benefits	Payroll Communication, Benefits Clarity	Understanding Compensation Structures, C&B Introduction Training
HR Policy & Compliance	POSH, Code of Conduct, Ethics, Audit Readiness	POSH, Code of Conduct, Workplace Ethics, Information Security
Employee Relations	Conflict Management, Grievance Handling	Conflict Resolution, Employee Rights, Grievance Redressal Training
Workforce Planning	Headcount Planning, Budgeting, Capacity Forecasting	Manpower Planning Essentials, Strategic Workforce Planning
HR Analytics & Reporting	People Dashboards, Insights Training, Data Interpretation	Data Interpretation for HR, Using HR Dashboards, Storytelling with Data
Organizational Development	Change Management, Culture Building, OD Interventions	Change Agility, Cultural Transformation, Leading OD Initiatives

HR Shared Services	Query Management, Internal Process Training, System Walkthroughs	HRMS Training, SOP Familiarization, Internal Helpdesk Etiquette
Health & Wellness	Mental Health, Safety, Ergonomics, Emergency Preparedness	Stress Management, Wellness at Work, Emergency Response Training

This list is an indicative thought on what areas you can speak about. Make sure you go prepared based on your organization's specific priority topics.

- **CTO**

CTOs often prefer building solutions in-house or choosing a solution that they can control for compliance purposes. And therefore, they must be approached carefully.

- **Do Not Sell a 'Software'**: CTOs are unlikely to be convinced by a feature list. Instead, discuss the **science of learning** and how the product embodies maturity, thought leadership, and psychological impact on employees.
- **Intangible Value**: Focus on how the product enhances employee experience and drives cultural change. These aspects go beyond technical metrics like server size or programming language.
- **Security Assurance**: One of the CTO's primary concerns is data security. Never enter this conversation unprepared. Present comprehensive answers to anticipated objections and demonstrate that security

is ensured at every stage of engagement. This is one objection: there is no work around it. The platform has to be secure as per industry standards. No deviations.

- **Procurement**

Procurement focuses on negotiations and showcasing value through cost optimization.

- **Challenge in Procurement**: Unlike other roles, this is difficult to crack. Their goal is to demonstrate negotiation success, not to assess strategic value.
- **Negotiation Strategy**: Understand that their target is to bring pricing down from a set starting point, regardless of prior discounts. Avoid over-negotiating before procurement enters the conversation, leaving no buffer for the partner.
- **Your Role**: Ensure sustainable, fair pricing from the beginning till the end. Clearly highlight which vendor you cannot afford to lose, even if procurement aims to push pricing further.
- **Disclaimer**: The science behind procurement negotiation remains complex and subjective. I am still learning to get around this one!!

DON'T BUY TECH BEFORE BUILDING CULTURE

1.8 "Don't Buy Tech Before Building Culture"

Get the People Onboard Before the Tech

Bringing in technology without cultivating a culture of learning is like buying a Ferrari for a city with no roads, it looks impressive, but it's going nowhere. The problem is rarely that employees don't want to learn or can't learn. It's often that the environment around them doesn't support or value continuous development. And that environment is shaped heavily by managers and their own mindset. Most organizations struggle with this reality.

Building the Culture Has 4 Elements:

1. Management Learning Mindset
2. Manager Learning Mindset
3. Learner Mindset
4. Tech Adoption

It's not uncommon to see managers themselves avoiding training programs, skipping courses, or even delegating course completions to juniors or administrative staff. Managers might prioritize day-to-day activities over learning, sending a strong message to their teams that training is not important. Employees then follow suit, taking pride in skipping training, which creates a toxic culture where development is sidelined, and growth, both personal and professional, comes to a standstill.

To fix this, you need more than just an LMS. You need a cultural shift, one where learning is viewed as a critical component of success. Without establishing this mindset, any investment in an LMS is just throwing money at a problem that won't go away.

Here's how to get the culture right before investing in tech addressing all the 4 elements:

1. **Lead by Example**: Managers must complete the same training programs they expect their teams to take. When leaders show that learning is a priority for them, it becomes a priority for everyone. This top-down approach ensures that learning is seen as valuable and essential.
2. **Set Clear Consequences for Lack of Engagement**: Establish clear consequences for both employees and managers who deprioritize learning. Communicate what they're missing out on, such as career growth opportunities, better project assignments, or even meeting compliance standards. If they understand what's at stake, they're more likely to engage.
3. **Incentivize Learning**: Recognize and reward employees and managers who actively participate in training. This could be through certifications, acknowledgments in team meetings, or even linking training to performance reviews. Rewards make people feel valued and can motivate those who are on the fence about engaging.
4. **Communicate the Value of Training**: Send clear messages about what employees and teams are missing out on by not engaging in learning. Highlight the growth, opportunities, and career advancement that come from completing these programs. Use real-life examples of employees who have benefited from training and how it has impacted their career progression.
5. **Align Learning with Business Goals**: Training needs to be relevant and directly tied to the current business challenges and employee roles. When employees see the connection between what they're learning and their job performance,

they'll be more likely to participate actively. This will ensure that training is not just a box-ticking exercise but something that contributes to their everyday work and future career.

6. **Address Resistance Head-On**: Identify managers who block their teams from attending training sessions, citing "busy schedules" or "urgent deliverables." Have direct conversations with these managers to show the impact of this behavior and discuss how L&D can work around the team's busy periods.
7. **Establish Accountability for Managers**: Make managers accountable for their teams' training engagement and completion rates. Set expectations and follow up with data. When managers know they are being monitored and that their support (or lack thereof) is visible, they are more likely to prioritize training.
8. **Adoption of Tech:** Without tech, the adoption to learning will remain limited. Educate employees to use mobile devices or the LMS app. For blue-collar employees, create classrooms with projectors and self-playing content. This prepares them to consume content effectively without trainers physically present.

Before investing in any learning platform, create a learning ecosystem that values and encourages growth. Otherwise, you're just pouring resources into a platform that no one will use effectively.

Run a free **LearnerMindset Assessment™** for your organization to get the score and some personalised tips that may be relevant to your organization. This is available on my personal website **gunjangupta.me**

> *Remember, technology alone won't transform your organization, people will. Lead the culture, nurture the mindset, and the LMS will become the tool that amplifies your impact, not the solution that fixes a problem.*
>
> **~ Gunjan Gupta**

LMS
Analytics
Social Learning
Virtual Training
Classroom Training
Elearning
Assessments

Chapter

02

Buying & Setting up the Right LMS

2.1 "Selecting The Perfect-Fit"

Not All That Glitters Is Gold

Cutting through the noise of flashy features. What really matters?

When choosing an LMS, most clients get dazzled by big names, fancy features, and high price tags. They assume that the most awarded LMS or the one with the longest list of features is automatically the best fit for their organization. I'm here to tell you: you couldn't be more wrong.

Think of it like choosing a car for your family. If you have a family of six, would you buy a luxurious limousine? Or maybe you'd go for the fastest car, like a Ferrari? Or perhaps the most expensive, renowned brand like BMW? These might be fantastic cars, but they're not going to meet your primary need: a vehicle with six seats that's practical for everyday use. So why treat your LMS purchase any differently?

SELECTING THE
PERFECT
FIT

Here's the truth: the biggest, most feature-rich LMS isn't necessarily the right fit for you. The focus should be on what you need, not what's trending in the market. Here's why:

1. **Features Don't Equal Fit:** The most expensive LMS with all the bells and whistles might have features you'll never use. Just like buying a sports car when you need a family vehicle, it's a waste. It's not about having everything under the sun; it's about having the right features that meet your immediate and near-future needs.
2. **Plan for the Next 5 Years, Not 10:** Businesses evolve rapidly. Trying to predict what you'll need 10 years down the line is like trying to drive blindfolded. Choose an LMS that will meet your critical expectations for the next 5 years, with enough scalability to handle foreseeable growth. After that, it's okay to reassess and upgrade if needed.
3. **Avoid Deadweight:** Don't carry around a bulky LMS that's over-engineered for your current state. If your company is just starting or still scaling, get a solution that fits your present scenario. You can always switch later when your needs change. Carrying a "limousine LMS" for a small team is just dead weight, you'll end up paying for features you don't use and acquiring a system that's simply not the right fit for your team.
4. **Scalability Matters, But Overplanning Can Hurt:** Ensure that the LMS can grow with you for at least 5 years. This means it should be flexible, upgradeable, and able to adapt to changes in your organizational structure. However, don't let the lure of future possibilities force you into buying an unnecessarily complex solution today.

5. **Be Clear About Your Use Case:** Define your use case clearly before getting swayed by the vendor's pitch. Understand your immediate goals, your employee's learning preferences, and what pain points the LMS needs to address right now. It's not about the LMS's popularity; it's about whether it can deliver results that matter to you.

   Large enterprises now realise this and it is a single reason why the top 1% customers in each industry choose to work with our organization.

   Focus on User Experience Over Flashy Features: It's easy to get caught up in a laundry list of features that sound great on paper but turn out to be clunky and hard to use. A simple, intuitive LMS that employees actually enjoy using will always beat a complex system that looks impressive but collects dust because no one wants to navigate it.

6. **Ask the Right Questions:** When evaluating an LMS, ask questions that cut through the hype. For example: "What's the average user adoption rate?" or "How often are feature updates rolled out, and at what cost?" or "How often do you patch when you realise there is a bug in the platform?" This will give you a clearer picture of long-term value versus just initial excitement.

7. **Don't Fear Outgrowing Your LMS:** It's okay to pick an LMS that serves you well for the next 5 years and then transition to another solution when your needs grow. Think of it like upgrading your car when your family expands, completely normal and expected.

8. **Total Cost of Ownership (TCO):** Evaluate the TCO, which includes not just the upfront licensing cost but also implementation, support, training, and future upgrades. A

cheaper LMS might end up costing you more in the long run if you have to pay for frequent upgrades or customizations.

9. **Future-Proof, But Don't Over-Plan:** Make sure the LMS has a solid roadmap and is backed by a vendor committed to continuous improvement. However, avoid overestimating your future needs, as business strategies can change faster than expected. Aim for flexibility, not an LMS that claims to predict the future.

No More Vendor BS: Asking the Hard Questions

Critical questions to ask vendors and what to look out for in the answers.

Every vendor will come at you with the same pitch: "We're the best in the market," "We have maximum features," or "The other product doesn't stand a chance against ours." They'll throw in a laundry list of all possible features, whether relevant or not, just to overwhelm you and make their solution seem like a perfect fit. But don't be fooled. Before you get lost in the vendor's jargon, it's crucial to approach the conversation with clarity and purpose.

Here's how to cut through the noise and get to what really matters:

1. **Define Your Requirements Clearly**

   Before engaging vendors, get your own house in order. Understand your organization's exact needs and break them down into key buckets:

   - **Compliance Requirements:** Does the LMS meet your industry's regulatory requirements? Can it handle mandatory training tracking and reporting?

- **Functional Requirements:** What specific functionalities do you need (e.g., content creation tools, assessments, integrations with existing tools)? Go as detailed as you can go. Eliminate features in the list that are not useful to your organization so you can focus on the critical features that you need.
- **Technical Requirements:** Is the platform compatible with your existing systems? What are the hosting options: cloud-based, on-premises, or hybrid?
- **Legal Requirements:** Does the vendor comply with data protection laws? What are the licensing terms? What happens to your data if you decide to exit?

2. **Don't Be Dazzled by Features:** It's common for vendors to list out all their features, many of which might not even be relevant to your business. Instead of being swayed by a long list of bells and whistles, focus on how each feature addresses your specific needs. If a feature doesn't contribute to solving your challenges, it's just unnecessary clutter.
3. **Ask Targeted Questions:** Prepare questions that reveal more than the vendor's standard pitch, such as:
    - "What's the average implementation time for companies of our size?"
    - "What are the most common reasons clients leave your LMS?"
    - "How frequently are updates or new features released, and at what cost?"
    - "What support options are available post-implementation, and what do they include?"

4. **Demand Transparency on Total Cost of Ownership (TCO):** Ask for a detailed breakdown of costs beyond the initial licensing. This should include implementation, training, customization, support, migration and any hidden fees. The vendor might gloss over these aspects, but knowing your TCO upfront will prevent surprises later.
5. **Validate the Claims:** Vendors often say, "We can do that" to almost any feature request. Challenge them to show you how. Ask for a live demo based on your use cases, not a generic product showcase. This will help you see if their claims hold true.
6. **Check Vendor Stability and Future Roadmap:** Make sure the vendor has a stable business model and is committed to evolving the product. Ask about their future roadmap, recent updates, and any planned upgrades. This will give you a sense of whether they're keeping up with industry trends and technology.
7. **Get References and Actually Call Them:** Most vendors will provide references who are likely to give glowing reviews. Ask for contacts of companies similar to yours in size and industry. When you speak with them, focus on real-world issues like implementation challenges, support responsiveness, and unexpected costs.
8. **Evaluate Vendor's Attitude Towards Customization:** Some LMSs are rigid and hard to customize, which can make them unsuitable for specific business needs. Ask how easy

it is to modify the platform to fit your unique requirements, and if those modifications are part of the standard offering or additional costs.

9. **Assess Data Security and Compliance Readiness:** Ask specific questions about data security measures, backup procedures, and compliance certifications (e.g., GDPR, ISO 27001). A good vendor will be transparent about their security protocols and compliance readiness.
10. **Investigate User Adoption Rates:** While most vendors boast about features, very few focus on user adoption. Ask the vendor about the average adoption rate across their customer base, as a low adoption rate could be a red flag that employees find the system difficult to use.
11. **Inquire About Migration Support:** Switching LMSs can be a logistical nightmare. Find out if the vendor provides assistance with data migration and how they ensure a smooth transition without disrupting your learning processes.
12. **Probe on Vendor's Customer Support Reputation:** Many LMS platforms falter when it comes to ongoing support. Ask questions like, "What is your typical response time for high-priority issues?" or "What support options are available outside standard business hours?" Quality of support is often a make-or-break factor.

Remember: Choosing the right LMS goes beyond the vendor's marketing pitch. The goal is to find a platform that truly aligns with your business needs and can adapt as your requirements evolve. I have often seen aggressive sales professionals promise a lot to close deals, but top management alignment on service and customization is critical, especially when you have important customizations.

AVOID THE HIDDEN TRAPS

Avoid the Hidden Traps

Hidden costs, lock-ins, and support disasters, know before you sign!

Choosing an LMS can sometimes feel like walking through a minefield, you think you're getting a great deal, only to find yourself hit by unexpected costs and constraints later. Here's where most companies go wrong: they get trapped by hidden costs, technology lock-ins, and support disasters that weren't apparent during the initial discussions. To avoid falling into these traps, you need to be vigilant and ask the right questions before you sign on the dotted line.

❖ **Hidden Costs: What You Don't See Can Hurt You**

One of the most common traps is hidden costs. These costs usually show up as you start customizing the LMS to fit your basic expectations. The issue isn't with wanting customizations; it's with not knowing how much those customizations will cost you.

Before finalizing your LMS selection, be very clear about what your **Minimum Viable Product (MVP)** is, what you absolutely need to go live, and what the costs around it look like. Here's what you should consider:

1. **Customization Costs:** How much will it cost to get your LMS to meet the MVP requirements? If you need custom reports, integrations, or specialized workflows, ask the vendor to provide a detailed cost breakdown.
2. **Recurring Costs:** What's the recurring annual cost, and are there any additional costs you need to be aware of? For example, licensing fees for advanced modules, increased storage, or per-user pricing for certain features.

3. **Additional Charges:** Are there undisclosed annual fees for maintenance, updates, or feature access? Some vendors won't tell you until after you've signed the contract, so be sure to ask directly during the evaluation stage.

4. **Implementation Fees:** Often, vendors will provide you with a license cost, but implementation, training, and data migration fees can be significant. Clarify these up front.

❖ Technology Lock-Ins: Getting Stuck in a Platform

Technology lock-ins can be disastrous if not evaluated correctly. A common scenario involves content creation tools that work only within a particular LMS and can't be exported to other platforms. For example, some platforms like Moodle use H5P for content authoring. While H5P content works seamlessly within certain ecosystems, it may not be SCORM-compliant, making it incompatible with other LMS platforms.

So, what happens if you decide to switch LMSs and all your content is tied to a proprietary format? You end up having to recreate everything from scratch, or worse, you're forced to stick with a subpar LMS because of the sunk cost.

What To Do:

➢ **Check Content Portability:** Ask if the content built within the LMS can be exported to a universal format like SCORM or xAPI. This will ensure that your content is reusable if you switch platforms.

➢ **Review Compatibility:** Make sure the LMS supports standardized content formats that can easily move between systems. If the LMS only supports its own proprietary format, consider it a red flag.

- **Minimum Commitment Lock-In**

Another trap is the minimum commitment lock-in. Some vendors enforce contracts that bind you to pay for a fixed number of licenses or a certain duration, regardless of whether the product is delivering value or not. You could find yourself paying for licenses that you're not using just because you're locked into a three-year agreement.

Example Case Study

ABC Mutual Funds Pvt. Ltd. (Name withheld due to privacy reasons!), invested in a popular LMS platform and signed a three-year commitment based on promises of a mobile app being rolled out. Despite repeated follow-ups, the vendor never delivered the mobile app, which was critical to the client's needs. When they decided to terminate the contract due to non-compliance, they had to pay a penalty for the remaining term. It ended up being a costly mistake that could have been avoided with clearer contract terms.

How to Avoid This

- **Ask for Shorter Initial Terms:** Negotiate for a maximum one-year initial commitment, giving you the flexibility to opt-out if the vendor fails to meet expectations.
- **Include Exit Clauses:** In case something goes sideways, ensure there are clear exit clauses in case the LMS doesn't deliver on key commitments, such as specific feature releases or support SLAs, you can walk out with no obligation beyond the current year.

❖ Support Disasters: Low Priority, High Risk

Support is often overlooked during the evaluation process, but it can become a nightmare post-implementation if not assessed properly. Most clients fail to ask critical questions about support, such as:

- "How many tickets do you handle daily in relation to the number of licenses?"
- "What percentage of tickets breach SLAs?"
- "What are the escalation processes and the vendor's response time for high-priority issues?"

How to Evaluate Support

To evaluate support properly, don't just take the vendor's word for it. Ask for a demo of their ticketing system and reporting capabilities. Request real support reports to see how they perform on their SLAs.

- **Get a Support Process Demo:** Like a product demo, ask the vendor to showcase their support ticketing system and how they track and resolve issues.
- **Request References on Support Quality:** When speaking to vendor-provided references, focus on support quality rather than just product functionality.

❖ Summing It Up

The best way to protect yourself is to have everything clearly documented during the evaluation stage. Outline your expectations, list non-negotiable requirements, and ensure the contract reflects what was promised. Here's what you can do:

- Be transparent with the vendor about your expectations and unique needs.

- Insist on seeing every detail in writing, whether it's support SLAs, costs for customizations, or product features.
- Plan for worst-case scenarios by including exit clauses that protect you, if the vendor fails to meet critical deliverables.

If you get all these points right, you'll set yourself up for a smoother implementation, fewer surprises, and a more successful LMS experience.

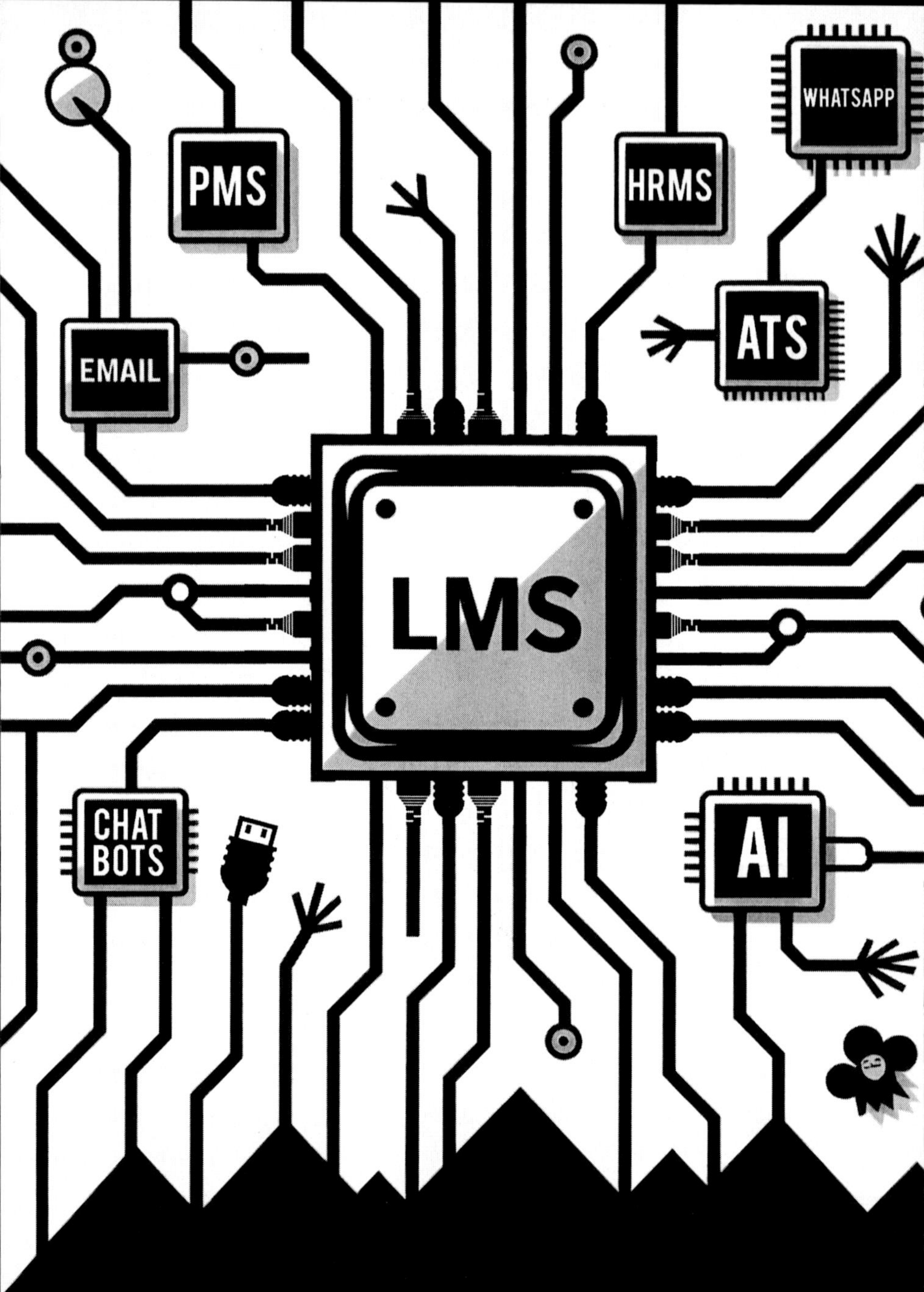

INTEGRATE OR DIE

2.2 "Integrate Or Die: Why Plugging In Is Not Optional Anymore"

When you read the title *"Integrate or Die"*, it may sound harsh, but it's the reality if you're building a learning ecosystem that needs to scale, adapt, and deliver results.

If your LMS sits in isolation, without connecting to your HRMS, performance systems, communication tools, or authentication mechanisms, it becomes a separate platform for users to remember. Every day your LMS isn't integrated is a day your learners are blocked, delayed, or demotivated.
It may start with something as small as a user not getting immediate access when they join or change roles. But these small issues add up, people drop off, completions fall, reports become unreliable, and soon, the platform is seen as inefficient or broken. This is how good LMS projects fail, not because the tool is bad, but because it doesn't *talk* to the rest of the ecosystem.

SSO, API & Real-Time Sync: Decoding Integration Levels for Scalability

- **Different Levels, Different Impact**: There are varying levels of integration. Some handle basic user sync, while others connect systems both ways. The stronger your integration, the lesser the friction for users and admins.
- **SSO is Non-Negotiable**: If you're still making users log in with separate credentials, you're hurting adoption. Single Sign-On is not a fancy feature, it tells the user that *this is part of your official work tools*.

- **Real-Time vs Batch**: If your user data or course completions update only once a day (or worse, weekly), that delay becomes visible. New joiners can't access mandatory training, promotions don't reflect in learning journeys, and the platform starts feeling outdated.

- **API-First vs API-Ready**: Some LMSs are built to connect (API-first); others can connect (API-ready). The former scales smoothly. The latter often means custom work, delayed timelines, and additional costs.

- **Manual Means Risk**: Anytime someone says, "We can upload Excel sheets weekly," you are introducing delay, risk, and human error. Manual integration is not a solution; it's a temporary fix.

- **Integration Isn't a Feature, It's a Foundation**: It's like plumbing. If it doesn't work silently in the background, you'll soon hear the noise and it will get messy.

- **Think Beyond HRMS**: Integration is not just about HRMS. Think MS Teams, Zoom, SMS gateways, WhatsApp APIs, Google Translate, Amazon Polly, Performance Management Systems, even your BI tools.

- **Avoiding Data Leaks and Compliance Headaches:** When integrating your LMS, ensure only essential data, required for user access, course assignment, and reporting, is shared. Sensitive information like salary, medical records, or personal history from HRMS should never be pushed to the LMS as it is not needed. Limiting data flow protects user privacy and prevents compliance risks.

I've mapped **over 32 integration areas** across client implementations, each one with measurable value. If you are as fanatical about integrations as I am, **drop me an email** and I will share my *Visionary Integration Landscape.*

GO LIVE,
BUT WITH A
GAME PLAN

2.3 Go Live, But With a Game Plan

Budget Busters: Know What You're Getting Into

- How to prevent your LMS project from becoming a money pit.
- Invest with separate budgets for content and platform.
- Identify if you need external content.
- Identify whether you need custom content or ready-made options.

As we've already understood the cost-related risks in LMS projects, it's crucial to plan the rollout with **360-degree preparedness**. This means recognizing that the platform alone won't create impact, you also need content, and a strong marketing and adoption strategy. Start by confirming whether your budgets for content and platform have been planned and allocated separately.

Content Budget Is Not Optional

When we talk about separating content budget from the LMS platform, remember, **a gun is useless without bullets**. If you want your LMS to deliver results, it needs content that's relevant for everyone.

A limited content strategy equals limited adoption. If other departments don't find content that speaks to them, they simply won't engage.

Where to source content

Next, decide whether you're building the content in-house or procuring it through third-party vendors. If outsourcing, choose vendors wisely. Many organizations fall for platforms like **Udemy,**

LinkedIn, Coursera, Percipio, Go1, or **Pluralsight**, drawn in by the sheer volume of content.

But volume is not the goal, **relevance is**. Map the content against your workforce needs.

- **Design Content for Everyone, Not Just One Function:** If you're aiming for organization-wide adoption, your content strategy must go beyond one function or department. One common mistake is focusing only on dominant teams like Sales.

  For example, if 60% of your workforce is in Sales, organizations tend to design product training, negotiation skills, or sales modules. But this leaves the remaining 40% disengaged due to irrelevant content.

  A limited content approach results in limited adoption.

- **Decide: Build In-House or Buy from Vendors:** Once you've planned for inclusive content, the next step is execution. Will you build it internally or source it from external providers? If outsourcing, be strategic. Many companies purchase access to large content libraries like Udemy, LinkedIn Learning, Coursera, Percipio, Go1, or Pluralsight.

  These platforms pitch their value through sheer volume, tens of thousands of courses, but quantity alone doesn't guarantee value.

  You must **map content to your audience's actual needs.** For example, if you're in IT or a technology-heavy sector, prioritize platforms that specialize in technical learning. Choose vendors who are first to publish new content, offer expert-led courses, include simulators, and provide practice environments.

While generic platforms may have some tech content, they may not go deep enough for your workforce. So choose vendors who offer **depth, relevance, and hands-on learning support** tailored to your business.

- **Integrated & Inclusive Content Strategy: Avoiding the Budget Black Hole**

  When identifying content for your organization, it's critical to budget for **platform integration**. Without it, users will see internal and external content on separate systems. Integrated content libraries allow learners to **track progress, search across resources**, and **experience unified learning journeys** that combine internal and vendor courses.

  One standout example involved a client using three platforms: **Udemy, Pluralsight, and LinkedIn Learning**, combined with internal content to curate rich, blended curriculums. Though a high investment, it delivered maximum impact because their business demanded it.

  However, **library content won't cover everything.** Essential modules like **Code of Conduct, HR policies, induction, or product training** are proprietary and must be **custom-created.** This is where clarity of vision matters, before jumping into development, define what kind of learning experience you want to deliver. Should it be gamified, feature Level-3 interactivity, or rely on simple video-based training?

  All these options come at different costs. To **avoid uncontrolled spending**, identify:

  - the **right LMS vendor** with integration capabilities,
  - the **right content partners**, and

- whether to build with **internal teams, external vendors, or a mix**.

Having created over 2500 courses for different audiences, I can assure you, **no single content partner fits all needs**. Evaluate thoroughly, plan for flexibility, and match content formats to your audience and business goals.

- **Set Realistic Timelines**
  - **No, You Can't Go Live by Friday – Create a Rollout Timeline That Actually Works:** One of the most common mistakes I see is assuming LMS deployment is just plug-and-play. It's not. You need to plan your rollout with clear, milestone-based stages, from vendor evaluation, internal approvals, and requirement finalization to UAT setup, content readiness, and the actual go-live. Each step takes time, and skipping any of them will only delay success, not speed it up.
  - **Build Two Plans – One from the Vendor, One from You:** The vendor will give you a project plan, but that's only half the story. You'll be running your own internal timeline in parallel, working with procurement, getting sign-offs, coordinating with internal SMEs, and managing content readiness. Both tracks must align for a smooth launch.
  - **Platform Ready, Content Missing – The Most Common Misalignment:** In too many cases, the platform is technically live, but the content isn't ready. Or the content is ready, but the LMS hasn't been configured. When timelines between platform and content don't sync, your launch impact drops. Avoid this by aligning

both early and making content part of the core project plan, not an afterthought.

(Note: Your billing starts as soon as one side delivers their part. Any delay from the other side will burn cost without adding value.)

- **Integrate External Content Seamlessly – Don't Create a Jarring Experience:** When you're buying third-party libraries, make sure they integrate into your LMS. A disjointed experience where internal and external content live in separate silos kills usability and tracking. The goal is unified discovery, progress tracking, and the ability to build blended journeys using both sources. I've worked with organizations using multiple platforms: Udemy, Pluralsight, LinkedIn Learning, Percipio, Zobble, and watched them weave everything beautifully with their internal content into one seamless curriculum. That's real curation, not chaos.
- **Don't Underestimate the Power of Custom Content – It's Your IP:** Some things just can't be bought off the shelf. Induction programs, code of conduct, HR policies, and product training need to be custom-built. This is your organization's DNA, and it demands attention. Whether you produce it internally or with a vendor, quality custom content adds unmatched value. And how you present it, from gamified modules to simple video formats, depends on your learning goals. Just remember, this is where most projects bleed money due to lack of clarity. Choose the right partners, set clear scopes, and match your content depth to your business needs.

- **Avoid the Black Hole of Budget Burn – Plan Your Content Path Early:** Creating content isn't a one-time task, it's an ongoing investment. To avoid draining your budget into a never-ending spiral, get clear early. Will you build internally or outsource? Will you need one vendor or a mix? In my experience, no single vendor covers all needs. Either you blend internal teams with partners, or use multiple content providers. Having built 2000+ courses tailored for learners worldwide, I can tell you, being open and thorough in this process saves time, money, and disappointment later. Evaluate content partners with the same scrutiny as your LMS vendor.

Closing Note

I am closing this book here, hoping you've found value in the insights I've shared. If you think there were things that you weren't aware of, or if this book helped you get a structured outline of the knowledge you already had, please do share your thoughts with me. I am open to feedback and eager to learn from each of my readers.

You might be lucky to have me add the success story to my next book or next edition.

It will be my win if you're able to:

- Convince your internal stakeholders with minimal objections,
- Understand your requirements better, and
- Choose a vendor that truly fits your organization's needs.

The next volume will focus on **marketing and adoption of the LMS**, because building it is just the beginning; making people use it is where the real game begins.

CRITICAL CHECKLIST
AND REAL-WORLD TOOLS
CHECKLIST
LMS

2.4 Critical Checklist and Real-World Tools

Final Toolkit to Transform Your LMS Journey

This isn't a bonus. It's 26 years of real implementation experience, mistakes, and breakthroughs, offered to you for free. Tools that clients have paid lakhs for are now available without a price tag.

Access all resources in one place:

LMSBlueprint.violetinfo.ai

LMS Readiness Checklist: A printable sheet to check if your team is truly ready.

Budget Buster Worksheet: A practical template to plan your costs, spot hidden fees, and stay on budget.

Avoid These Mistakes: Common pitfalls from real cases, and how to avoid them. Include case studies from different industries and problem statements.

32 LMS Integration Points: A downloadable list covering every real-world integration you'll need.

No-Fluff LMS Vendor Checklist: A clear, no-nonsense checklist to evaluate vendors and pick the right one.

Sample RFP Questions: Tough questions that help you filter out unnecessary promises from vendors.

Project Plan Templates: What a winning LMS rollout plan looks like, plus templates to help you execute.

L&D Glossary: Access all the keywords that you need to make sure you are ready to deal with people in the L & D function.

Join the TheLMSBlueprint Book Community : For HR leaders who want deep, distraction-free conversations.

Join the EliteLnD Group: For HR leaders who are ready to level up their journey. Exclusive paid access, but fully worth it.

A Personal Note

We Don't Just Build Products. We Engineer Experiences!

Let me be very honest here.

As I was about to finish this book, my team suggested creating a dedicated page to show readers what we offer. Honestly, at first, I hesitated. I worried it might make the book feel too salesy.

Then I discussed it with my mentor. He told me not to see it that way. He said this should be seen as a positive, a "Sone Pe Suhaga" moment. My readers have invested their valuable time, and it would be an injustice not to let them know about the tools and platforms we've built over the last two decades that can genuinely make a difference in their learning ecosystem.

So here it is. No jargon, no filler. Just what we do and why it matters.

We don't build software to tick boxes. We build it to untangle chaos, kill boring training, and solve the stuff that slows you down.

Platforms That Actually Work

- **VioletLMS:** When training feels all over the place, VioletLMS brings structure. It automates, tracks and tells you what's working.

- **VioletLXP:** Like a personal trainer for learning. It recommends what you need based on your job, your gaps and your goals.
- **VOnboard:** Helps new hires feel like part of the team even before they walk in. No more first-day awkwardness.
- **VAuthor:** Takes your boring old slides and turns them into gamified, interactive courses. Makes it an immersive learning experience through 20+ gamified themes.
- **VGamify:** Add fun to learning with badges, points, and leaderboards that actually make people want to finish their training.
- **VKnow:** Turns scattered knowledge into smart, searchable libraries. Built especially for BPOs and KPOs.

Our eLearning Experiences (Because LMS Alone Doesn't Cut It)

- **The Tough Talk:** Pick a character. Make choices that shape outcomes. It feels like a game but coaches you for real-world dilemmas.
- **The City Salvage:** Roll the dice, conquer challenges, and climb the scoreboard. A board-game style experience that tests your mind and strategy.
- **Off-the-Shelf Library:** 200+ micro-modules across soft skills, behavior, compliance, and safety. Ready-to-launch learning for every role, every need.
- **Custom Learning:** Bring your learning vision to life with courses built with ID Level 3 & 4 to suit adult learning. Custom immersive videos, gamified themes, and experiences that transform training.

AI Solutions

- **Adaptive Learning AI:** Harness AI to curate courses tailored to your audience profile — personalized, adaptive, and designed to resonate with every learner.
- **VConverse AI:** Practice tough conversations in a judgment-free space with an AI bot that listens, guides, and builds real confidence.
- **VELevate AI:** Empower your workforce with an on-demand AI coach that delivers accurate, policy-aligned answers as per your organization's workflow and processes.
- **VCommunicate AI:** Automate communication to drive learning with AI that ensures the right message reaches every employee, at the right time.
- **VGen AI Bot Builder:** Build assessment, onboarding, or learning bots in minutes. No coding, no delay — just smarter engagement.

Want to See Them in Action?

Drop an email to **sales@zobble.com** to explore all platforms, demos, and tools.

If you're ever evaluating LMS, LXP or onboarding tools, yes, we'd love to be on that shortlist. But more than anything, we love being part of problems that are worth solving.

Book Closed, Conversation Open

First, let me sincerely thank you for investing your valuable time in reading this book. Every page, every insight was shared with the hope that it helps you navigate your learning journey and make smarter decisions for your organization. Your time and attention mean the world to me.

I'd love to hear from you, your feedback, questions, or even just your thoughts on how these ideas could apply to your own context. If you're curious about exploring our tools, platforms, or learning experiences further, or want to discuss how we can solve specific challenges together, I'm here to connect.

You can reach out to me directly and even schedule a **1-on-1 conversation** to dive deeper:

gunjan.gupta@zobble.com

Thank you once again for reading. Here's to taking the next steps together!

Gunjan Gupta